DAVID SEAMAN

First published in 1997 by
Invincible Press
an imprint of HarperCollins*Publishers*
London



A CIP catalogue record for this book is available from the British Library.

ISBN 0 00 218820 1



Created and produced by Flame Tree Publishing,
a part of The Foundry Creative Media Company Ltd,
The Long House, Antrobus Road,
Chiswick, London W4 5HY.

Thanks to Jim Drewett, Alex Leith and the Deadline squad for their help in researching this book.

# DAVID SEAMAN

Introduction by Noam Friedlander
Main text by Philip Dodd

JVC

## CONTENTS

**THERE WAS** ONLY ONE hero during Euro 96: the safe-handed, strong-hearted goalstopper – David Seaman. Following in a distinguished line of goalkeepers, Seaman is the Hurst, Jennings or Shilton of our generation.

People will always remember Gascoigne's skill against the Scots, Teddy Sheringham's two goals against the Dutch, the dogged defensive skills of Tony Adams and fierce striking rate of Alan Shearer and likewise no one will ever forget Seaman saving goal after goal. England would not have made it to that epic semi-final against Germany without Seaman, but people tend to overlook the fact that he saved his team's skin by saving a penalty in the quarter-final shoot-out against Spain.

Seaman couldn't escape the media glare, even while attending a tennis match at Wimbledon. Waiting for a game to start, the whole of the Centre Court seating area erupted into a chorus of *Seaman, Seaman* and the tennis players had to wait to start their match. Football really had come home and Seaman was there to welcome it with open arms.

Although Seaman didn't win any medals with QPR, he was a vital member of their squad. Popular and dedicated, he was adored by the Rangers' faithful and valiantly kept their goal averages up. During the 1986-87 season, in one of the only games that Seaman did not play in, QPR lost to Sheffield Wednesday 7-1. Seaman is a man who likes clean sheets.

His most memorable game for QPR was probably on 19 November, 1989. Liverpool were gunning for another Division One Championship while QPR were floating in a mid-table position. When it came to the crunch, Seaman was there for the Super Hoops. Making an incredible acrobatic save, he tipped the Liverpool shot over the bar with his right hand – QPR beat the Champions 3-2. Seaman had triumphed once again.

QPR were reluctant to let him go, but George Graham's offer of a British record fee of £1.3m was too tempting for QPR to refuse. It was one of the biggest transfer fees that Arsenal had ever paid and the largest ever transfer fee for a keeper. So, during the summer of 1990, Seaman moved to the other side of London. Proving his £1.3m worth by being beaten only 18 times in his entire first season with the Gunners, he broke the club record for the fewest goals conceded. Arsenal lost just one League game all season – and won the Championship.

Seaman's popularity was such that he was voted the 1995-96 Player of the Year by the Arsenal Supporters' Club and they had good reason to give him the accolade. His heroic performances in Arsenal's two Cup Winners' Cup campaigns were the foundation for his club's success and the supporters love him. He'll never ignore the crowds, but acknowledges them with a wave and a smile, even during match play.

In spite of Seaman needing four painkilling jabs before his 1994 final against Parma, Arsenal still triumphed. So far with the Gunners, he has won a League Championship medal, a Coca-Cola Cup winners' medal, FA Cup winners' medal and European Cup Winners' Cup winners' medal. Furthermore, to date, he has been capped 36 times by England. Fighting off the challenges of Tim Flowers and Ian Walker, it is Seaman that England supporters demand to see in the goalmouth – he has earned the title of England's Number One.

**Noam Friedlander**

## YORKSHIRE BORN AND BRED

**IF THERE WAS** EVER ANY DOUBT about David Seaman's commitment to Arsenal, his deep love of football, or his sense of soccer history, you need look no further than just beneath his Arsenal or England jersey. The undershirt he wears, apparently for every game he plays in, is the very one that Bob Wilson, Seaman's goalkeeping coach at Arsenal, wore during the Gunners' glorious double-winning season of 1970-71. Yes, the season that still induces a fever pitch of laddish nostalgia amongst Highbury fans, the side that included George Graham, who as Arsenal manager signed David Seaman from QPR in 1990. The undershirt still sports Bob Wilson's initials.

By the end of England's brave Euro 96 campaign, David Seaman could count himself up there with the great Arsenal and England keepers of the past.

But his path to glory has not been straightforward. Of all the positions on the football field that of goalkeeper is the most exposed, the most vulnerable. Goalies rarely make the news, however good a save – Gordon Banks's 1970 classic from Pele is a rare exception – but one bad miss can linger for ever. The goalkeeper's primary objective is to prevent players scoring goals, and therefore gaining glory – it's a thankless task. Even Banks never quite scaled the same heights of public adoration reserved for Geoff Hurst, Jimmy Greaves and Bobby Charlton. Somehow a goal seems that much more tangible.

UMBRO
ENGLAND
1
reusch
GORE-WS
reusch
reusch
GORE-WS

Seaman has had his share of bad moments and public misses. But he has also securely lodged at least two saves – both from penalties – in the video memory banks and the grateful hearts of millions of fans.

Nature determined that David Andrew Seaman, born on 19 June 1963 in the South Yorkshire steel town of Rotherham, would be a goalkeeper. As a tall lad with a natural predilection for soccer, he was usually nominated to take up a position between the sticks for games at junior school and later at the local Kimberworth Comprehensive.

*They used to shout 'He's big, let's get him in goal'. I did have the odd game as a centre-forward but I was much better in goal.*

**David Seaman, *FourFourTwo*, 1996**

**HE CONTINUED** to grow – the adult Seaman is a large man, six feet four and a half inches tall, and fourteen stone ten. He'd make a handy rugby flank forward.

*He is huge every way you look at him, upwards, backwards, sideways. His hands, like paddles, rest on oak trunk thighs. He is dressed in a pale denim shirt with pale denim jeans which give the illusion of one great huge mass of blue.*

**Katherine Viner, *Sunday Times*, 1996**

**BUT IN SPITE** of being bigger than the other kids in class, he wasn't always able to demonstrate the goalkeeping skills that he would later develop by good training and out of a natural enthusiasm for the sport.

*It was my first game for my junior school. I played for the second half and let in 14 goals. We lost 26-0.*

**David Seaman, *FourFourTwo*, 1996**

**HE WOULD LATER** say that he sacrificed his schoolwork for football, and if he ever got into trouble his teachers, aware of his passion for soccer, would not bother to dish out detentions or extra work for David to do after school, but simply stop him doing PE.

He left school at 16, and was taken on as an apprentice at nearby Leeds United. Leeds were not the force they had been in the late 1960s and early 1970s, but they were still lodged firmly in the top half of the top division. It was a schoolboy dream come true: Seaman was a Leeds fan and had stood on the Elland Road terraces watching the manager, former Scottish international Eddie Gray, playing for the club.

His dream was short-lived. Seaman never played a senior game for Leeds: he was understudy to John Lukic, whose career was linked with his own again some 10 years later. In 1982 Eddie Gray told Seaman that he was not even good enough for the Leeds reserve team. Gray wanted someone 'more experienced'.

*It's a bit life-threatening really, because you're 19 and you've geared your whole life towards football, and somebody says you're not good enough, what am I going to do now?*
**David Seaman,**
***Sunday Times*, 1991**

**IT SEEMED** as though his career in professional football might be over and David started to look at alternative possibilities back in Rotherham. But his father had reminded him in true Yorkshire style that there was always another day – and a lucky break came his way.

Martin Wilkinson, who had been assistant manager at Leeds, moved to Peterborough, and remembered David Seaman. So Seaman joined the Posh on a free transfer and appeared for the club 91 times between 1982 and 1984.

From there he was sold to Birmingham City, where Ron Saunders was manager, for £100,000 in October 1984. Seaman enjoyed Saunders' support and encouragement, and later remarked that one of the plus points about moving to the club was that Ron Saunders knew quite a lot about goalkeeping... and was able to impart that knowledge.

*I went to Peterborough and I was just happy to have a job in football. Then I joined Birmingham and the afternoon I signed, all the press were there. I thought: 'Jesus, what's this like, a trial?' Ron Saunders said to them: 'This lad will play for England in three years.'*

**David Seaman, *FourFourTwo*, 1996**

**IN THE** event, Saunders was only a year out.

After two seasons and 75 appearances with the Blues, during which time he made 10 appearances in the England Under-21 team, Seaman moved down to London and on to Queen's Park Rangers in August 1986, signed by Jim Smith.

*QPR last night snapped up the man rated the best young goalkeeper in the country. Birmingham's Under-21 international David Seaman signed in a £225,000 deal at the Newport Pagnell service station on the M1.*
**John Etheridge, *The Sun*, August 1986**

# THE ROAD TO HIGHBURY

*Majed Abdullah gave David Seaman a start to his England career he will have nightmares about. His first real shot after waiting so long for his first cap and the QPR skipper could only get a left hand to Abdullah's effort and it crept agonisingly over the line.*
**Harry Harris, *The Mirror*, November 1988**

*Though David Seaman was seldom tested in goal, his performance was memorable only for an unconvincing punch and a shot that he touched but could not prevent from entering the net.*
**Patrick Barclay, *The Independent*, November 1988**

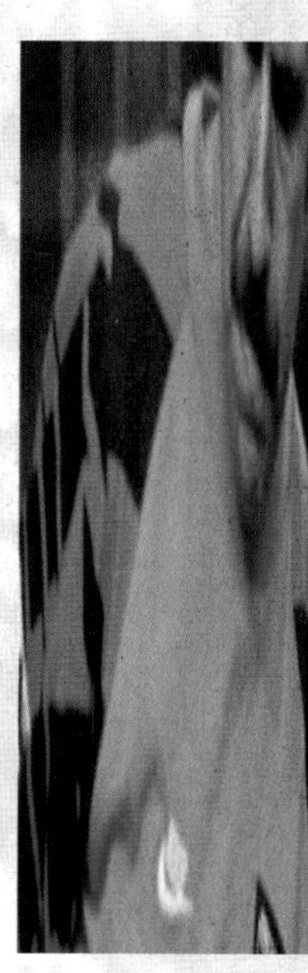

**DESPITE THE** disappointment, David was able to feature again in Robson's England sides, but only when Peter Shilton and Chris Woods were out of the reckoning. Seaman's second cap was as a substitute for Shilton who had set a new record of 109 appearances for England, and his third came against Czechoslovakia when Chris Woods bizarrely cut his finger on a penknife *while wrestling with the waistband of his tracksuit trousers.*

Back at QPR, now managed by Trevor Francis, the former England star and the first million-pound player, Seaman was able to demonstrate his skills. One save in a high profile 3-2 victory against FA Cup holders Liverpool in November 1989 caught the eye of all the journalists present.

*Liverpool are finding it tough going at the top for the first time under Kenny Dalglish. Francis saw his team produce a magnificent fighting performance.*
*Liverpool also found Rangers keeper David Seaman in inspired form and one save from Ian Rush in the second half was the best I have seen for years.*
**Brian Woolnough, *The Sun*, November 1989**

*Seaman had no chance with the Barnes left-foot shot that beat him after a dazzling run in the fifty-seventh minute. But then he seemed to have as little chance with the saves he did make, from Rush three times, from McMahon, from Houghton and from Molby. In the forty-ninth minute Rush was standing almost on the line when he deflected a McMahon header sharply and Seaman still got to it.*
**Frank McGhee, *The Observer*, November 1989**

**BUT OTHER** aspects of life at QPR were not going quite so well. Although Seaman's four seasons and 141 appearances (he barely missed a game) for QPR brought him wider exposure and top-flight experience, he was discouraged by the fact that the side rarely got TV coverage, had not won anything since the League Cup in 1967 and frankly looked unlikely to again. The infamous plastic pitch that was being used at Loftus Road also created particular difficulties for goalkeepers.

In addition there had been a certain amount of managerial turmoil. Trevor Francis, dubbed *too nice to succeed* by Brian Clough when he took over in 1988, was sacked the following year for being too tough. He had had a famous bust-up with Martin Allen when he demanded that the midfielder play against Newcastle rather than be with his wife at the birth of their first child.

And Seaman had fallen out with the management over the way negotiations were handled with George Graham at Arsenal, who was keen to sign the goalkeeper. Seaman was put on the transfer list, then taken off again, each time without being consulted.

*I was put on the transfer list without knowing, it was just we couldn't agree terms on the contract, and everything had to escalate from there. It was hard for me to play at QPR and get the stick off the fans.*

**David Seaman, *Sunday Times*, 1991**

**A SECOND** attempt fell through because John Lukic at Arsenal refused to move to QPR. But finally at the end of the 1989-90 season Seaman was transferred from Loftus Road to Highbury on 16 May 1990, for a fee of £1.3 million, equalling the world-record transfer fee for a goalkeeper set by Spanish club Seville who had paid the same for Russian international Rinat Dasaev in 1988. It was also Arsenal's biggest transfer fee ever at that point, although it effectively only cost Arsenal £300,000 since Lukic finally accepted a move back to Leeds for £1 million – the very team where Lukic had kept Seaman out of first team football at the start of his career! Sweet revenge indeed.

*Seaman finally became a Gunner yesterday, and admitted: 'My aim is to win the championship in my first season.'*
**Martin Samuel,**
***The Sun*, May 1990**

## WINNING THE FANS OVER

**WITH THE MOVE** TO HIGHBURY, Seaman was where he had wanted to be, at a big-name club that could offer him an ever bigger platform for his talents. His name had been linked with other clubs: it was reported that since Seaman's contract with QPR was due to expire in the summer of 1990, he could have signed with Glasgow Rangers or Manchester United, probably for even more money. But Seaman said that although he realised he could perhaps have earned more elsewhere, money came *a poor second to ambition*.

He told *The Sun: I think the big fee reflects the fact that managers are just beginning to realise how important a goalkeeper can be to his team. And I think I can live up to that fee. My job is to stop the goals that can get the League title back to Highbury.*

Becoming Arsenal's most expensive signing – George Graham's previous highest transfer fee had been to bring striker Alan Smith from Leicester City for £750,000 – might not have been a problem but Seaman had another issue to contend with: a hate campaign waiting for him among one section of the Arsenal fans.

John Lukic, who had been a key member of the Gunners' last-gasp Championship victory in 1988-89, had an extremely loyal following, and they were not best pleased at the way he had been ousted. After Arsenal's final game of the season at Norwich, supporters had demonstrated outside the team's dressing room for nearly 45 minutes, insisting that the club retain the keeper's services.

So Seaman took a certain amount of stick from the Lukic fans, but his broad shoulders shrugged off all their brickbats, and, by example, he won them round.

*It would have been easy for Dave to have ducked out. There were other offers and he could have taken them, but he chose Arsenal. The reason is simple – he wants to be the best. He wants to play for the best – and he feels Arsenal are the best.*
**Adviser Jerome Anderson, *The Mirror*, May 1990**

*It was my biggest worry, taking over from John Lukic. But they took to me quite quickly.*
**David Seaman, *FourFourTwo*, 1996**

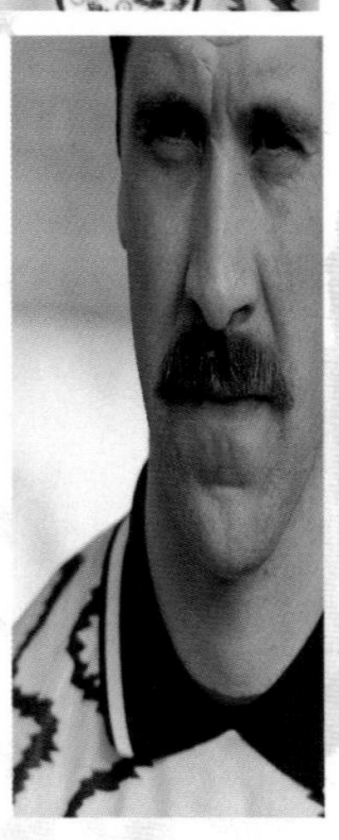

**HIS FIRST TASK** after joining his new club was to form part of the England squad travelling to take part in Italia 90. The only Arsenal member of the squad (even if he had yet to play for the Gunners), he had held off Dave Beasant for the spot as third-choice keeper behind Shilton and Woods. However, he saw no action as England progressed to the semi-final showdown with Germany. During a training session in Cagliari, England's base for the first round matches, his thumb was broken by a shot from Paul Parker, who had until very recently been a team-mate at QPR.

Once England's World Cup adventure had ended, David finally appeared for Arsenal in a tour match against Varbergs Bols of Sweden on 22 July 1990. It was a first, unpressurised chance to show his new manager whether he could deliver the qualities which had encouraged Graham to make Seaman Britain's most expensive goalkeeper.

*George Graham said he bought him for his courage, his elasticity, his command of his area, his mighty kicks into opposition territory, above all for what Graham calls 'his presence'.*
**Brian Glanville, *Sunday Times*, April 1991**

**DAVID SEAMAN'S** first League appearance for the Gunners was away at Wimbledon's Plough Lane ground on 25 August 1990, a match Arsenal won 3-0, but which failed to convince some observers that the £1.3 million had been money well spent.

*It may be club tradition or the caution of the manager, but it was difficult to mount a defence against Arsenal's decision to try and solve last season's scoring problem by spending £2.6 million on a goalkeeper and a centre-half in the summer. If conceding goals is a worry then there is a logic, but the defence was as tight as a jigsaw before. Which adds to the puzzle. Why replace John Lukic, who formed a strong part of that defence, with a keeper, David Seaman, who is arguably no better?*
**Martin Thorpe, *Guardian*, August 1990**

**SEAMAN STOPPED** the sniping in the most effective way possible, not only helping Arsenal win the 1990-91 Championship, but also by conceding a measly 18 goals in the whole season. When he'd left Queen's Park Rangers it had been his avowed intent to pick up a Championship winner's medal. A year later he did just that.

The parsimonious Arsenal defence broke the club record for the fewest goals conceded, and the side lost only one game in the campaign. The title was back at Highbury for the second time in three years, despite the deduction of two points earlier in the season for a pitch brawl with Manchester United – Seaman, typically, did not get involved in the fracas.

In one of the last games of the season, Seaman made a crucial contribution, preventing Sunderland from grabbing an 83rd minute winner, when he acrobatically tipped Gary Owers' powerful drive over the bar to preserve a 0-0 scoreline.

*David Seaman, the England keeper, whose brilliant late save at Roker Park climaxed a stunning first season in North London and virtually assures Arsenal can tie up the title tonight at Highbury.*

**Alex Mount, *The Sun*, May 1991**

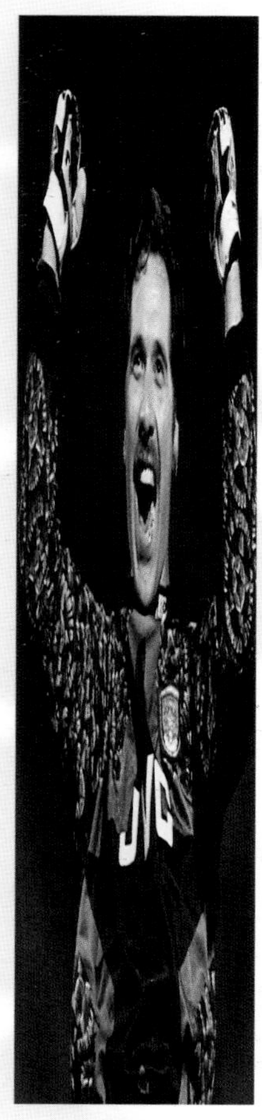

**WITH THE** Championship race coming down to the wire, only Liverpool could stop Arsenal, but the Anfield team were beaten 2-1 at Nottingham Forest, and the title went to North London removing all the pressure from the Gunners' match against Manchester United.

On the night Arsenal won 3-1, but Seaman brought down United's Mark Robins, conceding a penalty which Steve Bruce converted, denying David his 30th clean sheet of the season.

*'Christ, they've only lost one game! When was the last time that was done, a hundred years ago? It wasn't Liverpool, anyway'. He smiled at that.*

**Alex Ferguson, *The Independent*, May 1991**

**ARSENAL'S VETERAN** central defender David O'Leary, who'd seen many players in his Arsenal career (he holds the Highbury record for most appearances with 558 games), paid tribute to David Seaman in the keeper's first brilliant season at Highbury:

*He's the best in England. Simple as that. He doesn't get in a flap. Just deals with things without fuss and commands his box, which is tremendous. Nearest thing I have seen to Pat Jennings.*
**David O'Leary, *Sunday Times*, 1991**

## THE MEAN MACHINE

**THE CHAMPIONSHIP** CUP sitting proudly in the trophy cupboard at Highbury was concrete proof of the impact Seaman had made in his first season with the Gunners. The whingeing and moaning which had greeted his arrival had been silenced emphatically. But that first season was not all pure glory. Inevitably it was a missed save that was one of Seaman's most memorable moments. In the FA Cup semi-final against bitter rivals Spurs, Seaman was the barrier between the other North London club's aspirations for cup success after a barren period of nearly 10 years.

In a high profile encounter held at Wembley, Paul Gascoigne delivered the telling blow, a storming 35-yard strike from a dead-ball situation which went past Seaman like a cruise missile. The keeper just got a hand to it but only to help the ball into the top of the net.

One save he had made in an earlier cup tie at Highbury, against his former club Leeds, was one of the most spectacular of his career: a venomous drive was deflected not once but twice en route to goal. Still an airborne Seaman somehow managed to intercept the shot. It had been unleashed by one Gary McAllister: he and Seaman were of course due to meet in even more dramatic circumstances five years later.

In his first season with Arsenal, David also saw more international experience under new England boss Graham Taylor, including a February 1991 outing against Cameroon at Wembley. The temperature was freezing, and he had seen so little of the ball after the first 45 minutes that he held an impromptu warm-up with Peter Shilton out on the pitch during the half-time interval.

**THE FOLLOWING MONTH,** the Republic of Ireland made sure he had plenty more to go after, but Graham Taylor later criticised him, by letting it be known that Peter Shilton would never have let his defenders drop so far back – a comment that surprised many because it was so public.

Against Turkey in May 1991, Seaman pulled off a number of critical saves as England squeezed out a 1-0 victory with a Dennis Wise goal in Izmir.

*You can't call him a big-time bottler now.*
*His handling was assured, he made vital saves*
*and answered the call for more shouting at defenders.*
**Alex Montgomery, *The Sun*, May 1991**

**AFTER A FRIENDLY** with the losing World Cup finalists Argentina in the England Challenge Cup in May 1991, BBC pundit Jimmy Hill tipped him as the likely number one goalkeeper. Jimmy was wrong and Seaman only appeared twice in the next 27 internationals.

Meanwhile, following Arsenal's 1990-91 championship triumph, League success proved elusive for the Highbury club over the next few years – a fourth place was their highest placing. But the Mean Machine, the long-term back four plus Seaman in goal, retained the reputation they had earned in 1990-91 as the tightest, most consistent defence in what was still the First Division.

David was proud of the accolade, especially given the extra concentration demanded by the pace of play in the top flight.

*When you get to the First Division it gets harder. The balls aren't just knocked in, they're driven in with the purpose of making it harder for the goalkeeper to come for them.*
**David Seaman, *Sunday Times*, 1991**

**IF A STRIKER** did dare to penetrate the back four, he would be confronted by the massive figure of Seaman blocking the route to goal.

*When players come through alone on him, he is a wall.*
**Arsenal team-mate Anders Limpar, *Sunday Times*, 1991**

**SEAMAN** also applies himself to constant improvement of his trade: he tries to learn from every goal he lets in, watching match videos to analyse what went wrong.

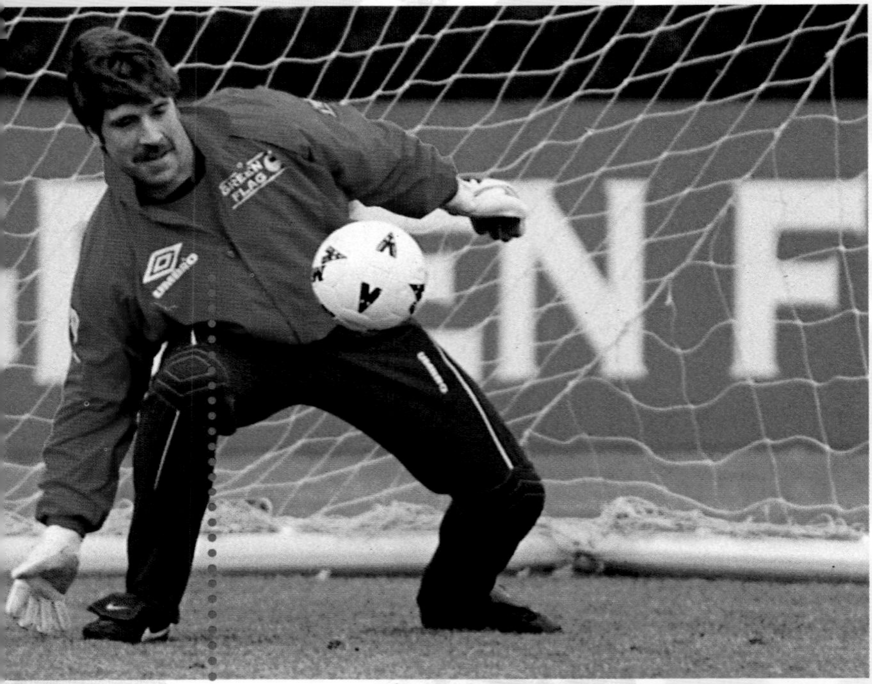
GREEN FLAG
UMBRO

ENGLAND
GREEN FLAG
UMBRO

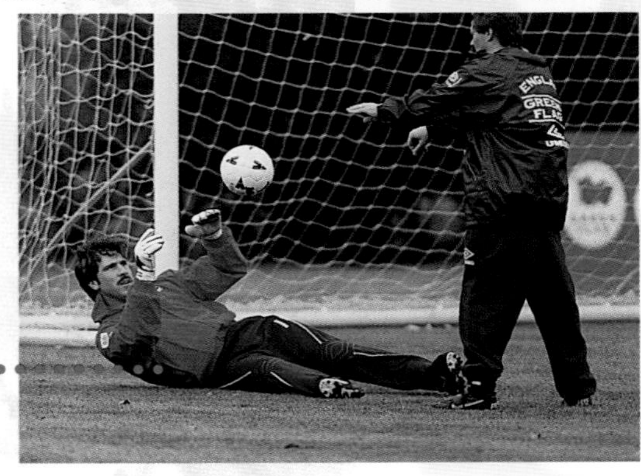

*I try to see why I got beat and if there is anything else I could have done to prevent it.*
**David Seaman, *FourFourTwo*, 1996**

*I still find I am being taught things by David Seaman. That's how good I think he is. Seaman is the ultimate student of the game, and he never ceases to amaze me in training.*
**Bob Wilson, *FourFourTwo*, 1995**

**BOB WILSON** describes goalkeeping as being based on three main areas of the body: the hands and upper body to catch, push or punch the ball away, the feet to make up ground quickly before committing to a dive or to narrow the angle of shooting, and the head for a sense of balance. According to Wilson, David Seaman has an edge over many of his rivals with his tough upper body strength. Hence his ability to deal with penalty shots.

His personality has a lot to do with it too. George Graham, like David O'Leary, used to compare Seaman to Pat Jennings, the great servant of both Spurs and Arsenal. Both are easy-going, quiet, unexcitable.

*There has never been an article written about Seaman that doesn't include the words 'phlegmatic Yorkshireman' (there you are, I've done it).*
**Amy Lawrence, *FourFourTwo*, 1996**

*It is how you handle those mistakes that is vital. I've made my fair share but I'm stronger in mind and body now. I am experienced enough to realise that in my position at the highest level you are usually depicted as either the hero or the villain.*

**David Seaman, *The Mirror*, 1997**

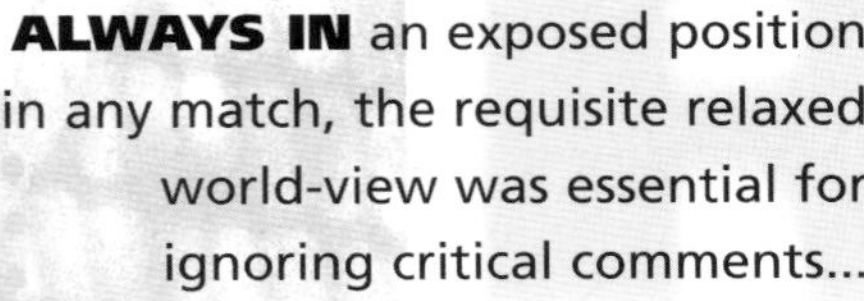

**ALWAYS IN** an exposed position in any match, the requisite relaxed world-view was essential for ignoring critical comments...

*This Spring, Arsenal's goalkeeper David Seaman is wearing a banana-yellow abattoir worker's smock with a fetching inlaid testcard motif, which is attractively repeated in a pair of radioactive side panels on his lycra-style shirts, for that fire-damaged tarpaulin look... Dumb grin, model's own.*

**Giles Smith, *Independent On Sunday*, 1994**

**MIND YOU,** in this instance, Seaman certainly agreed with the overall sentiment.

UMBRO
ENGLAND

*I don't like it full stop. Why do they have to make it multicoloured? A goalkeeper should look good, just a plain colour.*
**David Seaman, *FourFourTwo*, 1996**

**IF CHAMPIONSHIP** glory was not forthcoming after 1990-91, Seaman was still able to help Arsenal to FA Cup victory in 1993, beating Sheffield Wednesday after a replay, and completing a historic double whammy, since they had won the season's Coca-Cola Cup earlier in the season, also beating the luckless Wednesday.

*I remember a particular moment in the 1993 FA Cup Final when Seaman made a save from Chris Waddle. As Waddle turned away, the camera caught Seaman giving him a little wink. You can tell he enjoys the game.*
**Bob Wilson, *FourFourTwo*, July 1995**

UMBRO
ENGLAND
David
reusch
UMBRO

# KEEPING ON KEEPING ON

**AFTER THE** RETIREMENT of Peter Shilton in 1990 with 125 caps, an England record, the goalkeeping spot continued to oscillate between Seaman, Chris Woods and Tim Flowers, although Woods was effectively the number one choice.

Chris Woods realised how frustrating it was to be second pick. He had got into the England squad in 1984, and then had to sit out two World Cups and one European Championship while Shilton continued to rack up his tally of appearances. Woods said it felt as though Shilton had intended to go on for ever, and that maybe he would never get a long run in the England goal.

Now he fully intended to do the same, even though he realised this was tough on David Seaman. When Seaman did make it on to the team, he was not always successful. In 1992, for example, he earned the dubious, but for statisticians exquisite, record of becoming only the fourth England keeper to concede a goal direct from a corner!

More seriously, he was unable to establish his position in Graham Taylor's squad for the European Championships in Sweden in 1992, and was dropped entirely. He dealt with the setback in typical fashion.

*It devastated me. But sometimes you just have to bite your tongue and work harder to get back.*
**David Seaman, *The Sun*, 1993**

*Arsenal's man is a carp angler who has pulled out a 20lb specimen of our wariest fish. Such chaps can outwait Red Indians.*
**Mike Langley, *The Mirror*, May 1993**

**ENGLAND'S SORTIE** to Sweden had been disappointing, and Seaman at least could have a clear conscience about England's performance. In late 1993 he was finally given a chance by Graham Taylor to take part in England's bid to take part in the 1994 World Cup in the USA.

Meanwhile, there was time for a little light relief. George Graham remembers an unusual penalty moment that occurred in the 1993 Charity Shield against Manchester United. In the

week before the match, Ian Wright and David Seaman had been practising penalties, spicing up the training with extra points for the number of saves made or for scoring in the side netting. Then the pair would swop positions for a laugh. Seaman is blessed with a hefty kick and his strikes would leave 'goalie' Ian Wright's hand stinging for days afterwards.

When the Charity Shield went to a penalty shoot-out, Seaman volunteered to take one of the penalties:

*It was the worst penalty I have ever seen. Peter Schmeichel was lying on the floor waiting to receive the ball by the time it trickled into his grasp.*
**George Graham, *The Sun*, 1996**

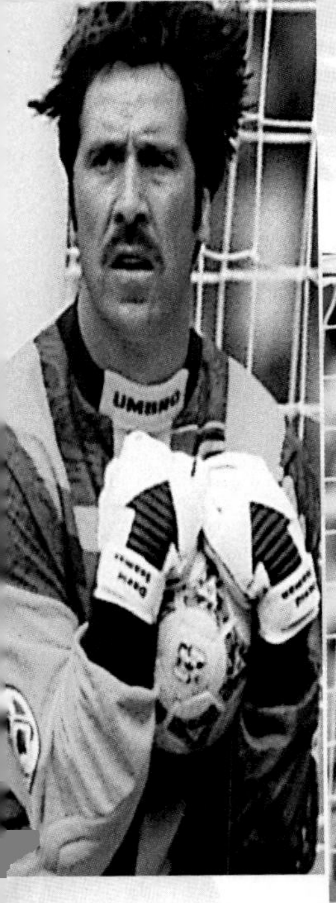

**SEAMAN'S MISS** cost Arsenal the match, and as he walked back to the centre circle, Graham was preparing to give him a serious piece of his mind. But as he looked at Seaman, he realised he couldn't – Seaman was laughing too much...

His World Cup campaign started well with a clean sheet against Poland, England winning 3-0 in September 1993, but foundered in the critical England v Holland match (*Do I not like orange*) on 13 October when deadball specialist Ronald Koeman beat Seaman from a free-kick. Koeman's first attempt had been a no-holds-barred thunderbolt, but Tony Adams raced out early and Paul Ince was booked as the free kick had to be taken again. Seaman had the first shot covered, but the Dutch had extended the wall for the retake and he was out of position when Koeman swopped power for precision, and delicately chipped the ball beyond Seaman's right hand.

*Again it's Koeman ... He's going to flick one now ... He's going to flick one ... He's going to flick one ... And it's in!*
**Brian Moore's TV commentary**

**GRAHAM TAYLOR'S** days as England manager were numbered (*Ta Ta Turnip* as *The Sun*'s headline gently put it), but one final humiliation was yet to come. Against San Marino on 17 November, at the Renato Dall'Ara stadium in Bologna, England – with David Seaman in goal – let in the fastest goal conceded by England in over 700 senior internationals, in front of the smallest crowd, a mere 2,378 souls, to watch an England match since 1883.

The damage was done in 8.3 seconds by Davide Gualtieri, a clerk for a San Marino computer firm. As the normally rock-like Stuart Pearce prepared to knock an attempted through-pass back to Seaman, he undercooked it completely, allowing the San Marino striker time to pick up the loose pass and drive a low shot past the isolated keeper.

England would not be making the trip to the States, but by the end of the ill-fated qualifying attempt David had successfully beaten off the competition from Chris Woods, Tim Flowers and QPR's Nigel Martyn to guarantee his place in new England coach Terry Venables' future plans.

Success in the international arena was nonetheless forthcoming for Seaman in the 1993-94 season, as he played a major part in Arsenal's triumph in the European Cup Winner's Cup. Pitted in the final against the existing holders, Parma, at the Parken Stadium in Copenhagen, Arsenal mounted a gutsy performance and defeated the favourites 1-0 through an Alan Smith goal, as the midfield clamped down the supply route to Parma's classy front line of Faustino Asprilla, Gianfranco Zola and Swedish international Thomas Brolin.

It was a victory achieved against the odds. Ian Wright was suspended, Jensen, Keown and Hillier were all injured, and David Seaman was suffering from painful rib injuries. In the previous season's FA Cup Final he'd played despite a double hernia (*No fuss, no truss, The Mirror* commented) and again he insisted on playing, keeping the suffering at bay with a series of painkilling injections. His interceptions were critical, getting his fingertips to a rapidly rising shot from Zola, and forcing Brolin to shoot against a post rather than into the back of the net.

*David Seaman is one of the most human people I know. He just fills the goal, fills it with his calm presence.*
**Bob Wilson, *Sunday Times*, 1996**

reusch
THE GUNNERS
Arsenal

reusch

## BACK FROM THE NIGHTMARE

**A YEAR** AFTER LIFTING the European Cup Winner's Cup in Copenhagen, Arsenal were back in the final – this time in Paris – to defend their title against Spain's Real Zaragoza.

In the last moments of extra time, with the score at one apiece, the game seemed to be moving inexorably towards a penalty shoot-out, both teams apparently winding down, ready to psych themselves back up for the pressures ahead. In the Arsenal camp, that prospect was not unduly daunting, as David Seaman had already made three penalty saves against Sampdoria in the semi-finals to assure Arsenal of their place in the final.

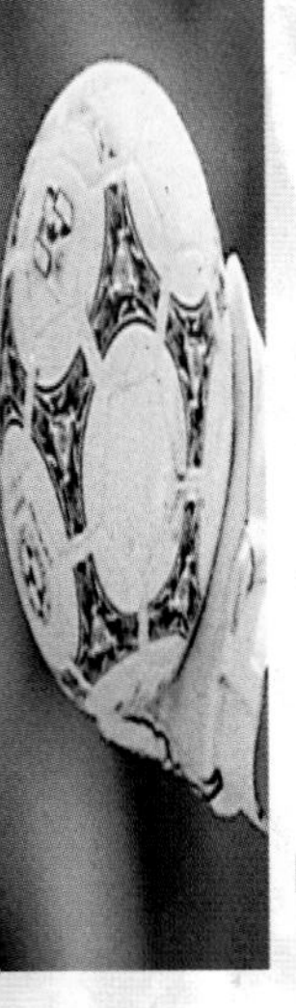

One man had other ideas. Nayim, the former Spurs player, picked up the ball around the halfway line. Fifty yards out, he looked up and noticed that Seaman had pushed out into a sweeping role, expecting that Arsenal would retain possession for the last few seconds. Nayim sent a lob high up into the floodlit Paris sky. It arced over the rapidly back-pedalling Seaman, who jumped, just too late, managing to get one hand to the ball, but unable to prevent it dropping over the line while he fell back into the net. As he knelt in the goal, his forlorn, anguished face was captured for every sports page the next morning.

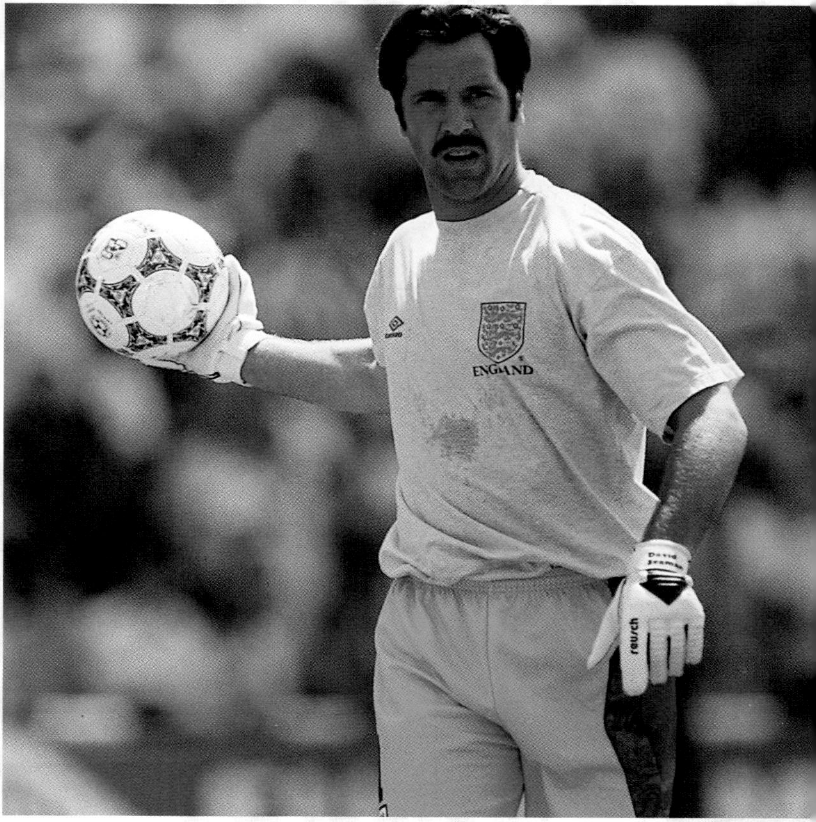

*As soon as I saw him hit it, I knew I was in trouble. I don't know what he was thinking but he meant it all right.*
**David Seaman, 90 Minutes, May 1995**

*The greatest goal I have ever seen. I saw Nayim look up and take aim. It was perfection and something I will remember forever. I doubt if football will ever see a goal like it again.*
**Paul Merson, *The Sun*, 1995**

*Of course I meant it. I spotted Seaman off his line and just tried it. I saw him out and he thought I was going to play it inside to Esnaider, so I whacked it.*
**Nayim, 90 Minutes, May 1995**

*When the whistle blew I was just looking for a hole to dive into. People came over to console me but I was in my own world and can't remember much about it. I really didn't know we were that close to the final whistle – when it went I just felt shattered.*
**David Seaman, *The Sun*, 1995**

**THERE WERE** tears in the dressing room, but captain Tony Adams gave his players a rousing speech to lift the demoralised team's spirits, reminding them how well they had done to have been seconds from retaining the Cup, and telling them they would be better and stronger as a result of the heartbreaking experience.

The memory of Nayim's goal in those fading seconds will be linked with David Seaman as long as people talk about football, but it is a measure of the man that he *was* able to shrug off the disappointment and come back stronger than ever. He still says he would take up the same field position again in the same circumstances, that Nayim's goal was a brilliant but freakish one-off.

**SPURS FANS** inevitably revelled in Seaman's misfortune. David was resigned to a season of jibes. Remembering Gascoigne's strike against him in the 1991 FA Cup semi-final and Koeman's free kick in the crucial World Cup qualifier against Holland, he might not have been blamed for thinking he was jinxed with players scoring spectacular goals against him on key occasions. If so, he later mused, it made up for all the times that strikers missed open goals from two yards...

*I know I am going to get it again when I walk out on Sunday. I am going to walk out to a chorus of 'Where were you when Nayim scored?' It is a fact of the goalkeeper's life. No one ever remembers the saves, they only remember the goals. The year Gazza scored against me, I let in 18 League goals all season. That never gets mentioned.*

**David Seaman, *The Sun*, 1995**

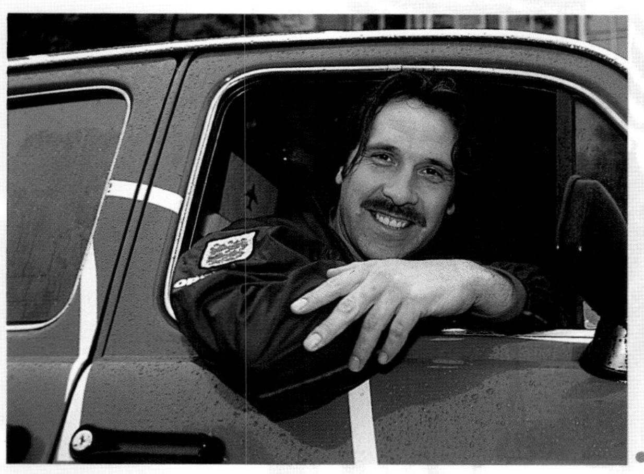

*We keepers have nowhere to hide when something like this happens. It is a test of character and I've no doubt David will bounce back.*
**Chris Woods, *The Sun*, 1995**

**SEAMAN'S** inbuilt sense of humour would be crucial in dealing with the disappointment.

*After David let in the Nayim goal in the European Cup Winners' Cup in 1995 there were many tears. But by the time he'd come off the plane at Stansted he was grinning and laughing again.*
**Bob Wilson, *Sunday Times*, 1996**

*He sounds like a bassoon player who has just heard the funniest joke in the whole world.*
**Amy Lawrence, *FourFourTwo*, 1996**

*I will always picture him in the middle of the dressing room laughing at the antics of the others. I always believed he was the perfect influence for jokers like Ian Wright. He was the one who laughs, he just stands there and laughs.*
**George Graham, *The Sun*, 1996**

**BENEATH DAVID'S** trademark moustache there usually lurks a beaming grin, the outward sign of his enthusiasm for the game. The first England goalkeeper since 1954 to sport a moustache, he shaved it off once – for a Leeds United team photograph – but decided it didn't look good and has kept it ever since.

*His dark hair is thick and glossy, like a coiffed man, the sort of hair someone from Rotherham might call poncy. But you don't argue with someone this big from Rotherham.*
**Katherine Viner, *Sunday Times*, 1996**

## THE LIONHEART

**TERRY VENABLES** HAD SHOWN his faith in David Seaman by including him in his first game in charge, against the European champions Denmark in March 1994. Venables kept him as number one for the next 18 games.

For the first time in his career he was the automatic first choice. After his third spot in the Italia 90 squad, the disappointment of not being selected for the 1992 European Championship and England's non-qualification for the World Cup in the States, here he was at last in place to perform in a major international tournament – and England, as hosts, didn't even need to qualify!

The England team's preparations for the tournament on a Far East tour caused palpitations among Britain's press corps, as Paul Gascoigne and the lads were photographed out on the town in Hong Kong, reclining on a dentist's chair as potent cocktails were poured down their throats. On the night in question, David Seaman was back in the hotel, asleep. (*I was gutted that I missed it though,* he said later. *It looked like a brilliant night out.*)

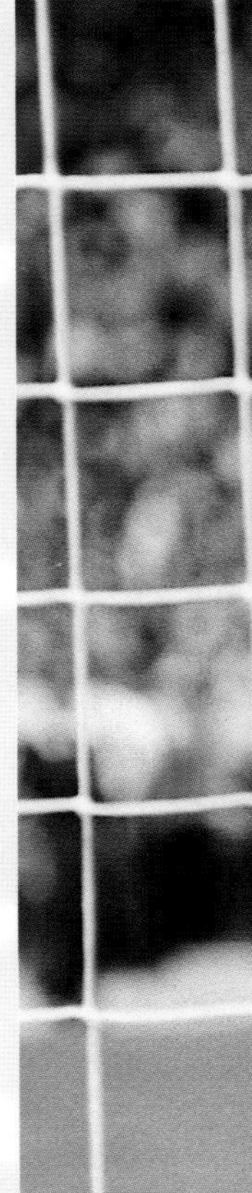

In the curtain-raiser for Euro 96, against Switzerland, it looked as if the team might still be suffering a hangover from the Hong Kong jollifications as they squandered Alan Shearer's 23rd-minute strike. Stuart Pearce was adjudged to have handled in the area and Turkyilmaz scored from the spot with seven minutes of the game left.

REDKNAPP
15

A week later, on a glorious summer Saturday, England took on Scotland at Wembley, the first time the auld enemies had faced each other for seven years, and David's first experience of the confrontation.

After a goalless first half, Alan Shearer's header from a Gary Neville cross had put England into the lead. Then the moment of truth came. After Tony Adams was deemed to have brought down Gordon Durie, Scotland were awarded a penalty. After the penalty conceded against Switzerland from the spot, English fans could only hope for a miracle, as Gary McAllister prepared to shoot.

It all happened in a blur. McAllister drove the ball straight, Seaman dived to his right but managed to connect his left elbow to the ball, which disappeared high and behind to the accompaniment of an eruption of relief from England supporters and a triumphant punch into thin air from Seaman. It was the only penalty save in open play in the whole tournament.

*Hitting it straight is not something I usually do, but given the stage of the game I felt I had to score.*
**Gary McAllister**

*Dates are everything in Anglo-Scottish history – 1314, 1746 and now 16:39. Forget Bannockburn and forget Culloden. In years to come students will be schooled in the precise moment Scottish forces were repelled by Lord Admiral David Seaman at Wembley on June 15. Seaman stood strong a mere 12 yards from the massed Caledonian cannons – and emerged with no greater injury than a tiny ball-mark on his left elbow.*
**Martin Samuel, *The Sun*, June 1996**

**SECONDS LATER** Darren Anderton had unleashed a ball to Paul Gascoigne, and with that deft touch of Gazza magic, the score was 2-0. It proved to be a turning point in the tournament, as suddenly the bad memories of Hong Kong and the opprobrium heaped on to the England team by the media evaporated.

*Gazza went berserk. He was shouting 'Yes!' at the top of his voice plus some things that were unprintable.*
**David Seaman, after the win against Scotland**

**THE SUN** reported that the next day the England camp had felt obliged to dispatch Seaman and Gascoigne to a trout lake to help calm down Gazza down: the two got on well, sharing their passion for fishing on England tours. Everyone remembered the penalty save from the match, but Seaman was in fact happier with an earlier save, when Gordon Durie, his head bandaged, had powered a header towards Seaman's left which the England keeper managed to claw away around the post.

*Saves do not have to be spectacular to be the best. It was a great low cross from John Collins. I knew I could not come out for it and so had to concentrate on what might happen. Durie was at the far post and got in a terrific header. I had to get a firm hand on it and just managed to stretch and push it out.*
**David Seaman, *The Mirror*, 1997**

**AFTER ENGLAND** had built on the Scotland victory by demolishing the much fancied Dutch team 4-1, their quarter-final opponents were Spain. An unyielding match gave few chances at either end, although Seaman made a spectacular tackle on Manjari 30 yards out of his goal. After extra time the score was tied 0-0, and it was down to penalties.

The tension was palpable. Stuart Pearce erased his own personal ghost and the memories of his semi-final miss in Italia 90 by slamming the ball beyond the Spanish keeper. Then, with the penalty score at 4-2, Miguel Angel Nadal came up to strike the ball, and Seaman clawed it away. Wembley erupted. The Seaman smile beamed like a lighthouse.

*The final heroic moment belonged, inevitably to Seaman, whose save from Nadal spared Fowler the angst of a further penalty. England's debt to their able Seaman grows and grows. At this rate he must surely end the tournament a rear-admiral.*
**David Lacey, *Guardian*, June 1996**

**IT WAS ENGLAND** v Germany again. The World Cup Final in 1966, the Italia 90 penalty nail-biter. Now after extra time, the score was locked at 1-1 – another penalty shoot-out. Seaman tried gallantly but could not find a third penalty save. He guessed the right direction three times, got his hand to Stefan Reuter's shot, but couldn't perform

the miracle to stop the winner from Andreas Moller hitting the roof of the net. He was quick to go and console Gareth Southgate as a stunned silence fell over the stadium.

*Perfection is rare in football or life. Arsenal's keeper came as close as anyone will in a major tournament. Not only was he England's saviour in penalty shoot-outs and at just about every other crucial time, he was the steadying influence on Paul Gascoigne.*
**Martin Samuel, *The Sun*, June 1996**

## SAFE HANDS

**EURO 96** brought David Seaman huge fame – an estimated 26.5 million Britons had watched the England v Germany semi-final clash. He was made absolutely aware of what he had achieved when he and Paul Ince went to Wimbledon to relax and watch some tennis. As they took their seats, the Centre Court gave them a standing ovation – and Pete Sampras was leading the cheering.

Quiet, modest, unassuming he might be, but David was relishing the attention on behalf of goalkeepers everywhere. He had really enjoyed the penalty shoot-outs, as he knew it was one of the few chances for a goalie to grab the headlines normally reserved for the strikers' union.

Best of all, the taunts from opposing fans had been quashed. The shared Euro 96 experience had transcended normal club rivalries and Seaman, along with the likes of Shearer and Gascoigne, could bask in a sense of national pride.

He had also gone a long way to achieving his intention to be the world's top keeper.

In July 1996 there was a rumour that Inter Milan wanted to sign Seaman and that Massimo Moratti, the club's millionaire owner, would personally finance the bid. Despite media talk of doubling his £12,000 a week salary, plus a lucrative golden handshake and a picturesque lakeside home, David stayed with Arsenal.

*I went into the finals as England's number one and was determined to be the best in the world. That was my ambition. I hope the saves I made and my performances enhanced my claim. I dispelled once and for all the whispers that when it comes to the big matches David Seaman doesn't have what it takes, doesn't have the bottle.*
**David Seaman, *The Mirror*, 1997**

TOURNOI DE FRANCE 1997

**WITH A NEW** England coach in the shape of Glenn Hoddle, he was the automatic pick for Hoddle's opening games with Moldova in September 1996 and Poland the following month, the latter England's first international back at home base after the semi-final.

David ended the year with official recognition of his contribution to the England campaign when he was awarded an MBE in the New Year's Honours List. But alongside the public acclaim 1996 also marked the end of his marriage to his childhood sweetheart, with all the personal heartache of breaking up a family – Seaman has two young sons. But he had a new romance, as the tabloids had been quick to uncover; the new love in his life described Seaman's charms.

*He's got it all: he's tall, dark and handsome, and that accent is just the icing on the cake.*

**Girlfriend, Debbie Rodgers, *Sunday Times*, 1996**

TOURNOI DE FRANCE 1997
ENGLAND
5

**BACK DOWN** to earth, Seaman's 1996-97 Arsenal season was badly hit by injury. He only made 22 League appearances, and missed a critical World Cup qualifier against Italy, a 1-0 defeat which looked as though it might set back Glenn Hoddle's aspirations. Ian Walker, in goal for the match, was criticised for his play, and needless to say, fans of David Seaman insisted that if he'd been fit he would have stopped Gianfranco Zola's shot.

One element of his career turned full circle when John Lukic returned to Arsenal from Leeds United on a free transfer. Fourteen years after David Seaman, as Lukic's deputy, had been given a free transfer to Peterborough, Lukic was now the understudy for Seaman, and as a result of David's injury made 15 League appearances for the Gunners.

In a March 1997 Premiership match against Liverpool, Seaman was involved in an unusual incident with fellow England international Robbie Fowler. Seaman came out as Fowler advanced on to a pass into the Arsenal area. Fowler tried to hurdle the approaching keeper but fell to the ground. Referee Gerald Ashby awarded a penalty.

Robbie Fowler immediately protested to the referee that Seaman had not fouled him – but the penalty decision stood. Fowler took it, a tad half-heartedly, and hit the post. Jason McAteer, following up, tapped the ball in from the rebound. Fowler's actions astonished most hardened cynics, took his team-mates by surprise, and prompted FIFA General Secretary Sepp Blatter to fax him personal congratulations on maintaining the integrity of the beautiful game.

By the start of the 1997-98 season David Seaman had appeared 249 times for his club, 36 times for his country, was safe in the affections of England supporters, still retained his reputation as the most secure keeper in the Premiership and could look forward to a potential appearance at the highest level in international football at the 1998 World Cup Finals – God, injuries, form and the right results willing.

It was a challenge the man who now signs autographs with the words 'Safe Hands' anticipated eagerly. He might still get nervous before a big match but his relaxed demeanour and modesty would stand him in good stead whatever the fates decided.

*The worst is before the game starts, when you go to have a look at the pitch in your suit and tie. But once I've got my kit on (my working clothes as I call them), then I'm alright.*

**David Seaman, on pre-match nerves, *FourFourTwo*, 1996**

*In a crowd of people I'll just keep quiet and hope no one notices me, which is pretty hard to do when you're 6ft 4in.*
**David Seaman, *Sunday Times*, 1996**

*There's only one goalkeeper remembered for a save – Gordon Banks. People need to learn to appreciate us.... They are slowly coming round.*
**David Seaman, *FourFourTwo*, 1996**

## FACT FILE

- *Full name*:
  David Andrew Seaman
- *Height*:
  6'4"
- *Weight*:
  14st 10lb
- *Born*:
  Rotherham 19 September 1963
- *Club*: Apprentice **Leeds Utd**. Then to: **Peterborough** (£4,000); **Birmingham City** (£100,000); **QPR** (£225,000); **Arsenal** (£1.3million).

- In May 1990, Arsenal paid QPR £1.3 million for Seaman, breaking the British keeper record – previously set at £1 million when Crystal Palace bought Nigel Martyn from Bristol Rovers.
- 1990-91 season Arsenal lose only one of their 38 League games - the smallest number of defeats in League history for 102 years (when the season only consisted of 22 matches and Preston remained unbeaten). With David Seaman on board, the Gunners remained undefeated for 24 matches before losing to Chelsea at Stamford Bridge 2-1, (2 Feb 1991).

### CAREER

- Snapped up in 1990 by George Graham after Arsenal released John Lukic.

- Collected his first Championship medal at the end of the season.
- 1990-91 season Seaman conceded only 18 League goals.
- Euro 96 special – David Seaman received his second Man of the Match award.
- Renownedly England's No. 1 & International goalkeeper.
- 2 superb penalty saves in Euro 96 (v Scotland & v Spain).
- Club Honours: Div 1 91; FAC 93; FLC 93; ECWC 94.
- FA Cup winner 1993.
- League Championship medal 1991
- Coca-Cola (League) Cup winner in 1993.
- European Cup Winners' Cup winner in 1994.
- European Cup Winners' Cup runner-up 1995.
- England player of the year 1996 (due to his awesome keeping during Euro 96).

## SEAMAN & ENGLAND

- *15 June 1996*
  Saves a penalty from Scotland's Gary McAllister – England win 2-0.
- *18 June 1996*
  With Seaman in goal, England storm into the last eight in Euro 96, after beating Holland at Wembley.
- *22 June 1996*
  Seaman clinches England's victory in the quarter-finals of Euro 96 by saving a penalty from Spain's Miguel Nadal.
- *27 June 1996*
  England win UEFA's Fair Play Award for Euro 96.

## TRANSFERS

- Leeds Utd apprentice 22 September 1981
- Peterborough Utd 13 August 1982 for £4,000: FL 91; FLC 10; FAC 5
- Birmingham City 5 October 1984 for £100,000: FL 75, FLC 4, FAC 5
- QPR 7 August 1986 for £225,000: FL 141; FLC 13; FAC 17, Others 4
- Arsenal 18 May 1990 for £1.3m: F/PL 227; FLC 28; FAC 30; Others 26

## HONOURS

- 1996 England Footballer of the Year Trophy
- MBE

## INJURIES

- On 16 October 1996, Seaman suffered broken ribs after an Arsenal defeat by Manchester United. The injury kept him off the pitch for six weeks.

## ARSENAL

- Ground: Highbury, Avenell Road, Highbury, London N15 1BU.
- Ground capacity: 38,500.
- Pitch measurements: 110 yd x 73 yd.
- Year formed: 1886 (joined the League in 1893).
- Founder: Daniel Danskin.
- Former names: Dial Square; Royal Arsenal; Woolwich Arsenal; 'The' Arsenal.
- Former stadia: Plumstead Stadium; Sportsman's Ground; Manor Road; Invicta Ground; Manor Road.
- Nickname: 'The Gunners'.
- Current sponsors: JVC Electrical.
- Greatest rivals: Tottenham Hotspur (the 121st & 122nd meeting of the two sides in this year's Premiership).
- Celebrity fans: Melvyn Bragg, Nick Hornby, John Lydon, Damon Hill, Clive Anderson, Paula Yates, Frankie Dettori & George Carey.

- Fans' favourite: Ian Wright.
- It's True: London Underground were persuaded to change the name of the nearest tube station to Arsenal back in 1932 by the manager Herbert Chapman. The inlaid signs on the platform walls still have the old name: Gillespie Road.
- Weirdest merchandise: Bibs for babies and the Arsenal all-over body-spray.
- Management history: George Allison 1934-47; Tom Whittaker 1947-56; Jack Crayston 1956-58; George Swindin 1958-62; Billy Wright 1962-66; Bertie Mee 1966-76; Terry Neill 1976-83; Don Howe 1983-86; George Graham 1986-95; Bruce Rioch 1995-96; Arsene Wenger 1996.
- Greatest score: 12-0 v Loughborough Town (Division Two, 2 March 1900).
- Record defeat: 0-8 v Loughborough Town (Division Two, 2 December 1898).
- Leading goalscorers (then/now): Ted Drake 42 goals (Division One 1934-45 season) / Ian Wright 30 goals (23 League, 2 UEFA Cup & 5 Coca Cola Cup 1996-97)
- Record Transfer paid: £7.5 million for Dennis Bergkamp from Inter Milan June 1995

- Record Transfer received: £3.2 million (rising to £5 million) for John Hartson (West Ham United)
- Record attendence: 73,295 v Sunderland (Division One) 9 March 1935
- Major honours: League Champions 1930-31; 1932-33; 1933-34; 1934-35; 1937-38; 1947-48; 1952-53; 1970-71; 1988-89; 1990-91. FA Cup Winners 1930; 1936; 1950; 1971; 1979; 1993. UEFA Cup winners 1969-70. European Cup Winners Cup 1993-94. League Cup winners 1987 & 1993.
- Best website: http://arsenal.co.uk (the offical one) & http://netlink.co.uk/users/arseweb/

- In 1994, Arsenal striker Paul Merson revealed he has an alcohol and drug addiction. In September 1996, he was recalled by manager Glenn Hoddle.
- On 1 August 1996, Bruce Rioch finally signed a contract as Arsenal manager after 14 months in the job — he was waiting for the club to countersign it. On the same day, Borussia Dortmund's Patrik Berger's signing was completed.
- On 12 August 1996, Arsenal sacked Bruce Rioch (after 61 weeks in charge). He is the shortest-reigning Arsenal manager in the club's history.
- Later in August 1996 it was revealed that Arsene Wenger was to take over as manager.
- In September 1996, Arsenal suffered a shock and humiliating tabloid experiences as captain Tony Adams admitted to being an alcoholic.
- Five year Premiership record: 3rd (1996-97); 5th; 12th; 4th; 10th.

## THE CURRENT SQUAD

- Goalkeepers: David Seaman (English international with 36 caps) previous clubs Leeds United, Peterborough, Birmingham City & Queens Park Rangers. Alex Manninger (Austrian international Under-21) previous clubs Vorwarts Steyr, Casino, Salzburg & Casion Graz. Signed for £500,000. John Lukic (English international England B, Under-21 & Youth). Previous club Leeds (twice). Vince Bartram (English Schools international) previous clubs Wolverhampton Wanderers, Blackpool & Bournemouth. Signed for £400,000.
- Defenders: Lee Dixon (English international with 21 caps) previous clubs Burnley, Chester, Bury & Stoke City. Nigel Winterburn (English international with 2 caps) previous clubs Birmingham City & Wimbledon. Steve Bould (English international with 2 caps) previous clubs Stoke City & Torquay United. Tony Adams (English international with 48 caps). Signed as a Trainee. Martin Keown (English international with 15 caps) previous clubs Arsenal, Brighton & Hove Albion (loan), Aston Villa & Everton. Resigned with Arsenal after a gap of 7 years for £2 million. Gilles Grimandi (French) previous club AS Monaco. Remi Garde (French international with 3 caps) previous clubs Lyon & Strasbourg. Matthew Upton (English Youth international) previous club Luton Town. Signed, initially for £1.2 million rising to £2 million. Scott Marshall (Scottish Under-21 international) previous clubs Rotherham (loan), Oxford (loan) & Sheffield United (loan). Gavin McGowan (English Youth international). Signed from Trainee but loaned to Luton Town at start of the 1997-98 season.

- Mid-fielders: Patrick Vieira (born Dakar but a French international and Under-21) previous clubs AS Cannes & AC Milan. David Platt (English international with 62 caps) previous clubs Manchester United, Crewe, Aston Villa, Bari, Juventus & Sampdoria. Ray Parlour (English international Under-21). Signed from Trainee. Emmanuel Petit (French international with 5 caps) previous club AS Monaco. Luis Boa Morte (Portuguese international) previous club Sporting Lisbon. Signed for £1.75 million. Ian Selley (English Under-21 international). Signed from a trainee. Alberto Mendez (German) previous club FC Feucht. Signed for £250,000. Paul Shaw (English) previous clubs Burnley (loan), Cardiff City (loan) & Peterborough (loan). Stephen Hughes (English Under-21 international). Signed from a Trainee.
- Wingers: Marc Overmars (Dutch international with 33 caps) previous clubs Go Ahead Eagles, Willem II & Ajax. Signed for £7 million. Glenn Helder (Dutch international with 4 caps) previous clubs Sparta Rotterdam & Vitesse Arnhem. Signed for £2.3 million (George Graham's last signing).
- Forwards: Ian Wright (English international with 27 caps) previous club Crystal Palace. Nicolas Anelka (French international Under-21) previous club Paris St Germain. Denis Bergkamp (Dutch international with 48 caps) previous clubs Ajax & Internationale. Signed for £7.5 million. Christopher Wreh (Liberian international) previous clubs Guincamp (loan) & Monaco. Signed for £300,000. Chris Kiwomya (English Under-21 international) previous clubs Ipswich Town & Le Havre (loan). Signed from Ipswich for £1.5 million.
- Who's Bad: Ian Wright (one red & ten yellow cards last season).
- One To Watch: Steven Hughes.

Introduction by Noam Friedlander.
Noam Friedlander worked as an intern on the CNN International Sports Desk in Atlanta. Since then, she has worked on the *Sunday Times* Sports Desk, *The Box* magazine and the *Manchester United Official Review 96/7*. She is now a freelance journalist and contributes to *FourFourTwo*, *Glory,Glory Man United* and Manchester United magazines.

Main text by Philip Dodd.
Philip Dodd is a writer and publishing consultant specialising in popular culture, including sport and music. In 1996, he was the publisher of *The Virgin Book of Football Records*. He is a lifelong supporter of Ipswich Town, through the good times and the bad.

Fact file compiled by Jon Sutherland.

The Foundry would like to thank Helen Burke, Helen Courtney, Helen Johnson, Lucinda Hawksley, Lee Matthews, Morse Modaberi and Sonya Newland for all their work on this project.

Picture Credits
All pictures © copyright Empics Sports Photo Agency